A SHADE
I CANNOT NAME

poems by

Carol Traynor Mayer

Finishing Line Press
Georgetown, Kentucky

A SHADE
I CANNOT NAME

Publisher: Leah Huete de Maines
Editor: Christen Kincaid
Cover Art: Jason Goldstein, jasongoldsteinphotography.com
Author Photo: Jason Goldstein, jasongoldsteinphotography.com
Cover Design: Elizabeth Maines McCleavy

Order online: www.finishinglinepress.com
also available on amazon.com

Author inquiries and mail orders:
Finishing Line Press
PO Box 1626
Georgetown, Kentucky 40324
USA

Contents

For my family.

*The value of life lies in the power of contemplation
and not mere survival.*
—Aristotle

CYPRESS GROVE IN A COLD SNAP

No longer green, broad leaves of *Alligator Rush*
chafe and rub, which sounds like water rushing.

When we stroll the raised walkway, silence
for better or worse save a lone animal's

banshee-like cry mingled with muffled gunfire.
Knee-deep, the watershed beneath drifts

in broad sheets west to the Gulf's warm mouth.
A chill lingers long in us. As if an afterthought,

ferns grow in rows on fallen Cypress trunks
giving us something to discuss.

Note, air plants nestle in limbs
as a way of living without risk.

EACH MAN MAKES HIS OWN SHIPWRECK

Short on sunlight, with months of bitter
cold, wild blueberries rim his bungalow.

A swamp maple, summertime, shades
an inconsequential patch of yard.

Father dies soon. We can all start over
unless we won't.

Dust mingles silent in his sunlit
shed, unceremoniously unlatched

by a jury-rigged rope. Crossed rake
and hoe, a wooden X. I steal

a three-legged copper buffalo
paperweight, its uncanny impulse to fall.

EVER THE SAME

Swift brook, wide with rain,
drags scrawny twigs downstream
which resemble arms adrift.

He pots a Red Japanese maple
seedling dug up on a June
evening walk. His hands
best deep in soil.

Submissively, wisteria girds
the trellis. Dandelions anchor
wherever they please.

Our elderly neighbor's car
comes and goes, by this
we know him to be alive.

FROM MY OWN APARTMENT

Thickets of thorny brambles
climb a steep rise to the street,
and from here, an uncertainty
as to which plant each branch
belongs. I walk naked
room to room in moonlight,
a body past being wanted.

Light grey sky should drizzle
and be done. The stream within
the park, black green, gives
an illusion of depth.

My forks and knives stacked
off-kilter like felled, helter-skelter
Sycamores in the park below: a game
with sticks children played, I
remember on a circular braided rug
and there was no real winner.

ARMSTRONG KELLEY PARK

The fir's dumb
to the tree
trimmer's weight
and woody balm
freed after each
dismemberment.

Through a freshly opened
clearing, the town
power station hulks.

White plastic bag
snagged on scarlet
burning bush, a flag
of sorts. Gangly
rhodies hold fast to
tear-shaped buds until
the cardinal again,
turns rust to red.

LAW OF THE LAND

Through December, trees wear
Autumn. Rock Creek rushes
swiftly south this morning.

Its small pool by dawn,
mellow, no longer meshes
with foam. Leaves matted flat,
kindling in wait.

A Spanish Revival across
the ravine, granite path connects
us, closed to the public.

Workers abandon the job
for winter, that isn't winter
at all. The wild of these
woods in between, hardly wild.

DUE EAST OF THE OYSTER BEDS

In the shucked corn's toothless,
mealy ear, my grandson
comes to know death. A bug bite
festers on his left temple.

The drug addled townie pedals
fast past *Fancy's Market*. Its listless,
striped awning slopes drowsy
above the broad green door.

How I long to leave my mark
like the mottled moth stuck
to our hot tar roof. In its stead,
a fixed silhouette, a scar.

MY SISTER'S PAINTING OF OUR CHILDHOOD HOME

We all live in a house on fire
      —Tennessee Williams

Our house, set square in the forefront
in the manner of a primitive.

Stairs meet a screened front door
with no hint of a dog wagging inside.

Liberties taken with greenery suggest
a surrounding meadow or glen.

Why paint a single tree denying
the dense shade normally cast?

You must imagine that in real life,
the constant sirens were not silent.

EASTER SUNDAY

I brood on our bike ride.

Forgot to light Passover candles,
last year's melted wax, blackened
wicks pinned sideways,
like·necks held down by boots.

Trinity-By-The-Cove lets out.
Floral cross, proof Jesus's risen.

Tonight's sunset gave all it had.
The bay's a grave for the half-sunk
ship, waves that feather outward.

Marsh rabbits made a comeback.

Monday, men will pound hammers
to rebuild what's wrecked.

SPIRIT OF PLACE

Glistened hulls, well into sunset.
April falls again. Trawlers hunt
bass, stripers, along horizon's spine.

Marsh runoff, ruled by the moon
changed course over March.
Sedge meted out just enough
months to grow, then yellow.

Whose barn is being built? Idle
excavator at daybreak, a predator
in wait. Sand bluffs tower
cross bay, leave the chance
for landslide ajar.

Why the four-lane bridge to here
has no railings seems a mystery,
lest people prefer it that way.

PEDESTRIAN BRIDGE OVER GORDON RIVER

Community Hospital's striped smokestack
under monotony of mid-day glare
smolders with body parts.

He speaks in a monotone candor
of the long-married about a litany
of my flaws, that brands me

much like the manatee's scarred
back we spot as it ambles
under the pedestrian bridge.

The tension of its body
slowly surfaces to fan
outward parallel circles

which flatten and fall short
of mangroves that witness
the world grow old.

LIFE CHANGED, NOT TAKEN AWAY

Step through a door frame
since the screen's out for repair.
Our pantry's no longer bare.
We settle in for six months
until the next interruption.

Oaks leaf overnight, a sleight
of hand. Pollen wafts in
yellow-green bands, gets
the best of us.

A whitish threadlike matter
settles on shoreline muck
giving the appearance of a spider
web. Must everything be likened
to something else to matter?

Dark neck and head of a cormorant
glides elsewhere above water,
its body secreted away.

RINGLING MUSEM

Backlit, sun off Biscayne Bay,
a shade I cannot name. Spanish
moss hangs from parking lot
sycamores. Blackbirds, already North.

Don't ask how its feels to lose
my friend, not knowing
she neared death.

Mary breastfeeds Jesus
in *The Flight into Egypt*,
owes nothing to cherubs above.

Cottonwood canopies rustle,
shed white seeds far and wide
like wind-driven snow.

SNOW BIRD

Dips in sand post-storm appear
immutable like the blue tattoo

of Gibran's *The Prophet* on my
esthetician's voluptuous body. She

speaks of her love for Lorca
the way you speak of God.

Regular goings on of tufted
white birds lap the sunset horizon.

January around the corner,
brims with drier air.

Palm trees lit for a holiday
I care nothing about.

TO THE STARS

Here, hydrangea, pinkish white,
planted for my liking. Bikes
in the garage, tinkered with.
At day's end, the radioactive
green hummingbird's
breast suspended, mid-flight,
in the name of sustenance.

My husband guesses
at constellations. His breath,
warm, as the metal hull
of a slow stroked *Arrow* canoe.

Now, murky sky ever murkier,
entering the long silence.
Two cottontails up from their warren,
nibble purple clover. What they devour,
won't grow again.

TRESPASS

My kids flew back home, left
me with twice the loneliness.

Discovered an empty rodent burrow
on a dusty road two doors down

midst a tangle of cat o'nine tails.
I bemoan picking wild pink roses

there. The many cuts on my hands,
I don't see coming.

Long grass dangles from the gutter
like lithe wisps of rope.

Hallway paint, *Ponder White*,
takes on a dark mask at night.

WEIGHT OF ALL THINGS

Time to get on. Evening bones
stiff and sore suit me.

A vole
offers up its cry.

Squirrels heedlessly undermine
tulips. Headless stems, relics.

Pitch pines aim to seed then starve
an abandoned cranberry bog,

What's left
of its reedy vines?

Serpentine ribbons of fog
sift over a brick post office.

The world ends
at my fingertips.

Carol Traynor Mayer is a poet of place. Traynor Mayer shapes her imagistic verse from parts of her life spent in Washington, D.C., and the varied saltwater landscapes of New England where she always finds solace. In 2021, she founded the program, Words That Burn, and leads free poetry-writing workshops for teens to foster greater self-awareness and better understanding of the world. *A Shade I Cannot Name* is her first collection.

www.ingramcontent.com/pod-product-compliance
Lightning Source LLC
Chambersburg PA
CBHW022109080426
42734CB00009B/1535